Creating with Batik

Ellen Bystrøm

VNR VAN NOSTRAND REINHOLD COMPANY
New York · Cincinnati · Toronto · London · Melbourne

This book was originally
published in Danish as BATIK
– TEKNIK OG IDEER by Høst &
Søns Forlag, Copenhagen

Copyright © Ellen Byström and
Høst & Søns Forlag, 1972
English translation © Van
Nostrand Reinhold Company
Ltd. 1974

Translated from the Danish by
Christine James

Library of Congress Catalog
Card Number 72 9720
ISBN 0442-29974 5

This book is set in Optima and
is printed in Great Britain by
Jolly & Barber Limited, Rugby,
and bound by the Ferndale
Book Company, Ferndale,
Glamorgan

Published by Van Nostrand
Reinhold Company Ltd.,
25–28 Buckingham Gate,
London SW1E 6LQ, and
Van Nostrand Reinhold
Company Inc., 450 West 33rd
Street, New York, N.Y.10001

Published simultaneously in
Canada by Van Nostrand
Reinhold Company Ltd.

16 15 14 13 12 11 10 9 8 7 6 5 4 3 2 1

Contents

Preface

Batik work has become very popular in recent years. Many people have some knowledge of working methods and realize the wide possibilities offered by this form of textile decoration.

This book is written mainly for those who have some experience of batik and are past the beginner's stage. It is hoped that the book will encourage its readers to explore to the full the possibilities of free creative work.

So that beginners are not left out in the cold however, short sections are included in which the basic principles and methods are explained. These also serve as revision for those rather further advanced. In the remaining sections, every effort has been made to point out opportunities for introducing variations and experiments with colours and forms.

The examples given in the book are intended to stimulate independent and creative experimentation, so that technical knowledge does not become an end in itself but is used as a means of expressing the personality and abilities of the individual. Do not regard the illustrations as patterns to be imitated.

The author would like to thank Gunhild Jørgensen, batik teacher, for her practical help and advice in the writing of this book. I would also like to thank my colleagues Ida Harsløf, Kirsten Lundberg, Liselotte Palsdal and Gudrun Schmidt for their interest and assistance in preparing the material.

ELLEN BYSTRØM

Theatre dolls from Java in batik dresses. These dolls are about 70 years old.

Introduction

The origins of batik are obscure. The work itself comes from the East Indies. Java is the most famous for batik work but it is made on all the islands and is used for everyday clothing and for special festive costumes. The art was brought to Europe by the Arabs; intitially, it is thought, to the Spanish island of Majorca. Later the technique was adopted by the silk mills of Switzerland and Lyons.

Fragments of batik work have been found in Egyptian graves more than 2,000 years old. Amongst these was a man's head-dress known as *ikat kapala*. It has been established that the Egyptians used an unusual method of batik; covering and dyeing yarn before weaving it into cloth.

The word batik includes a wide range of methods of applying coloured designs to textiles. All these methods involve the resist principle, which means covering over parts of the fabric with various things so that those parts do not dye when immersed in the dye bath. This is the central feature of all batik work. The result is a

white negative pattern on a coloured background. A subtle effect is achieved if one proceeds to dye the white portions in other colours.

The methods and effects of resist dyeing are various. Tie-dye is a technique of folding cloth, tying and binding it to produce characteristic patterns. It originates in Java where it is known as *plangi*.

Closely connected with tie-dye batik is *tritik*, the name being the Indonesian term for this particular method of resist dyeing. It is done with a needle and thread, the pattern being formed by drawing the lines of tacking together. This kind of batik also makes use of the technique of sewing or knotting into the fabric various materials such as rice, balls of various sizes, or fruit kernels. Patterns are then formed, irrespective of the shape of the article used, when the fabric is dyed.

Another method is to cover areas of material with wax to protect them from dye. When this protective covering is not completely effective, a little dye will penetrate, which will appear as a form of cracking. At one time this was regarded as a fault in batik work, but nowadays the effect is deliberately sought. In fact it is actively encouraged by breaking the layer of wax.

A particular batik effect is obtained by drawing thin protective lines of wax with a *tjanting*, allowing great freedom in producing completely individual patterns.

Prerequisites for work

For good results you need time to work painstakingly and methodically at the different stages of batik production, regardless of what technique is involved. It is a combination of care and method that will produce the best results.

It is wise to make a habit of keeping sketches and notes. Record particulars of suitable resists, dyes and chemicals used, and the dyeing time needed to produce certain colours. Dye samples to test for colour and design effects. If you wish, these can be of a size that could be put to some practical use. Regard samples as a basis for fresh work.

When you are working with a number of articles at once prepare them all before dyeing. If for any reason it is necessary to mark the articles, attach an agreed number of small safety pins to one corner.

If it is important to note down particulars about dye baths, fix labels to the bowls with clothes pegs.

Collect together all the necessary equipment before you start work. Use containers that will not rust or corrode. Plastic, enamel and stainless steel bowls and pans are ideal.

Suitable materials

Use natural materials such as cotton, unbleached calico, batiste, satin, cambric, terry towelling, voile, velveteen, curduroy, taffeta, wool and silk. Special non-iron or impregnated materials are not suitable. Choose materials suited to the articles you wish to make. Cotton is most naturally suited to batik work, but it is advisable to select fairly coarse cloth for large curtains and tablecloths, and finer, smoother fabrics for articles of clothing.

The surface of the material is of prime importance as it will affect the method you choose in executing your design.

The size and thickness of the material determine how much dye will be needed. Calculate the total weight of the material and allow 4 to 6 pints (2 to 3 litres) of dye bath per 4 oz (100 g).

Washing out dressing

Regardless of what kind of material you choose, it is absolutely essential that it should be free of dressing. Dressing acts to some extent as a resist in itself and prevents dye penetrating the fibres. Natural silk is always free of dressing.

Test all other materials by pouring either a drop of diluted potassium iodide or a drop of lugosol solution on to a corner of the fabric. It will turn blue if any dressing is present. Both solutions are obtainable from chemists.

Wash out the dressing in a bath of lukewarm water adding a handful of soda for every 2 pints (1 litre). Ensure that no chalky residue clings to the material. Finally wash again in warm soapy water. Bear in mind that cotton material tends to shrink by about 10 per cent.

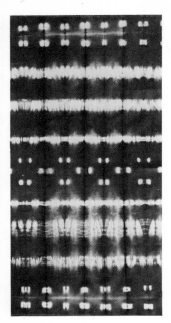

Sample showing several different methods of tie-dyeing. (See also the drawing on page 12.)

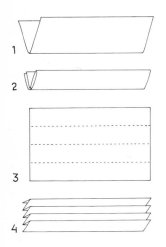

Accordion pleating.

Tie-dye batik

As an introduction to the art of batik, tie-dyeing is a relatively simple and distinctive technique. It can lead to completely free and creative work, since it offers many possibilities for experimentation. All methods of binding with thread and string can be linked and varied to produce individual pattern rhythms. Restrict yourself at first to small articles such as place mats, napkins for bread baskets, handkerchiefs and scarves, and for each article use only one method of tying. You will then have a series of basic patterns. Later you can use these ideas in larger compositions or designs for paper patterns.

A simple fold illustrating tying techniques

Folding is best done with an iron, but can be done by hand. Damping will help to give sharper pleats. A particular method of folding, accordion pleating, is discussed here. Others will be illustrated throughout the book.

First fold the material systematically to make a succession of basic lines and fields which will be a help in the final folding. (See drawings 1, 2 and 3.)

Drawing 4 shows the actual folding of the material where the long fields are divided once again, and the material folded to make accordion pleating.

The number of fields the material is divided into depends on the size of the material and the pattern desired.

The tying of the material can be done in a number of ways. Some of the possibilities are shown here on one piece of material as a basis to work from.

The numbers below refer to the figures on the drawing.

Method 1

The folded ends of the material are turned over at one end, covered with pieces of rubber which are bent round the sides of the material and held in place with small plastic clothes pegs. The pegs must be pushed well home, so as not to fall off in the subsequent dyeing of the material.

Rubber from a car tyre is suitable. Cycle tyres can also be used, provided they are cut to fit the size of the pegs, otherwise they will be likely to curl up.

Decide for yourself what size and shape you want to cut the pieces, but remember not to make them too big in relation to the pegs, or some of the dye will penetrate. Large pieces of rubber may be attached with two or more pegs.

The pegs must be small, so as not to take up too much space in the dye bath, and made of plastic so that they will not absorb the

dye. Wooden pegs cannot be used more than once, as they give off some of the dye from the first bath. On the other hand, rubber and plastic pegs may not stand boiling, so use with vat dyes only.

Method 2
Isolate the field with strips from a nylon stocking. Bind the material tightly and tie with an ordinary knot.

A brush or bottle-cleaner can be used for sprinkling the material with water before folding.

Method 3
Bind 2½ in (50 cm) of thick string firmly round the material without straining. The ends of the string can be fastened in several ways. See drawing for both the binding and tying of the string. Variations

Pressing the folded material. Use a thin wooden ruler to keep the pleats accurate and ensure that they are marked right through the material. Don't use a plastic ruler!

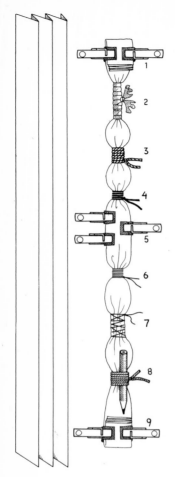

of pattern are not caused by different thicknesses of string, but by the tightness of the binding.

Method 4

1½ in (40 cm) of thin string is bound tightly round the material. The loose ends are not tied in a knot, but caught in a loop from the last time round (see drawing 2).

If the article is dyed in a number of baths, there may be occasion to remove some of the binding between the baths. You can then use the loose ends as a marker to show how much of the binding to remove. Sections in the middle of a length of binding can also be easily found and removed in this way (see drawing 3).

Method 5

Here pieces of rubber are used as in method 1, except that the pieces are half the size, and they are placed on both sides of the material just inside the edge, before the pegs are fixed.

The illustration on page 13 shows how a pattern rhythm can be built up by attaching one piece of "resist" material above another on the folded material.

In larger pieces of work the distance between the pieces of resist material can be varied.

Method 6

Bind white linen thread tightly round the material. As this thread is finer than string, quite thin and characteristic lines may be produced. The binding should not be too wide. Black linen thread is not recommended, as it marks the material.

Method 7

Bind white linen thread criss-cross round the material, once in each direction. This gives a sort of network effect, provided one remembers to work over these parts carefully in the dye bath. First bind the thread once round the material and knot it. Leave the loose ends hanging. Then start the criss-cross binding, and to finish off tie the two loose ends together.

Method 8

If you wish for a transitional shade between the colour and the white– negative– pattern, you can lay a pencil-end underneath the string binding. Remove it as soon as you have tied the ends of the string. This gives a consistent loose binding, which is otherwise difficult to achieve. The binding should be a little broader than usual, as the dye will work in more easily under a loose binding than a tight one.

Method 9

So as to make the sample usable as a table runner, the two ends have been treated the same way. This helps to give balance and

Sample showing different kinds of folding and tying. The finished work is shown in the illustration on page 10.

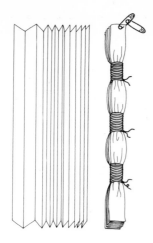

The accordion pleated material is tied to produce a regular striped pattern. Note safety pins for marking.

harmony to the very irregular bands of pattern in the middle. However, a different resist has been used. Double strips of material under the plastic pegs generally produce the same effect as pieces of rubber, and can be used as an alternative.

If you work with larger pieces of material such as curtains, it is necessary to cover the outer surface of the fabric with pieces of material before tying, to prevent it from absorbing too much dye.

Different ways of fastening the end of the binding thread.

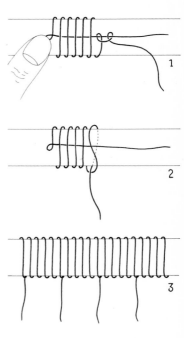

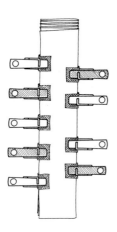

Folded material with pieces of rubber from cycle or car tyres attached by clothes pegs.

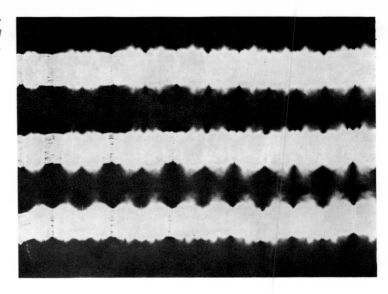

Preliminary bath before dyeing

When the material has been tied, put it in a preliminary bath of hot water. The water must be hot so that the material will not cool down the subsequent dye bath. In order to open the fibres of the fabric and help the water to penetrate quickly, add Lissapol D and soak for half an hour. This also helps the dye pigments to penetrate the material.

Folded articles ready to be dyed with instant dyes.

Dyeing with instant dyes

If you want to experiment with batik work without expecting a very high standard of colour-fastness, you can do so easily and cheaply using ordinary instant dyes which can be bought anywhere – Dylon Liquid, Dylon Multipurpose, Rit, Drummer etc. These will dye most light coloured fabrics with the exception of man-made fibres.

The Solamine range of dyes are fast to sunlight but the dyeing process takes up to an hour.

The method is largely the same for the two types of dye.

You will need:
The chosen dye
A plastic bucket
A large and a small saucepan
A piece of greaseproof paper (for crushing any dye in tablet form)
A piece of rag
Salt

Folding to form a cone.

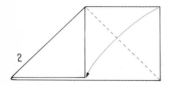

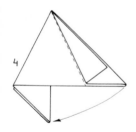

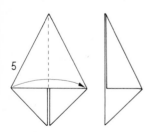

Most of these dyes are sold in quantities sufficient to dye 9 oz (250 g) of material dry weight. Instructions are given with the dyes. A brief outline of the procedure is as follows:

Place the dye powder in a pan and mix to a smooth paste with a little water. Make up to 2 pints (1 litre) with boiling water. Fill a large pan with 1¾ gallons (7 litres) of lukewarm water for every 9 oz (250 g) of material to be dyed. Add the dye solution, plus one tablespoon of salt for each capsule used. Carefully squeeze the soaked material and boil it gently in the dye for 15 to 20 minutes, or longer for deeper tones. Stir constantly. Rinse thoroughly in cold water and dry.

To prevent undissolved grains of dye spoiling the design, the powder can be tied up in a small piece of rag.

Reactive dyes

Reactive dyes are so called because they only work when a solution of salt and soda is added to the dye solution and a chemical reaction takes place.

There is a good range of colours in Dylon Cold and Procion M

Two batiste scarves dyed with instant dyes.

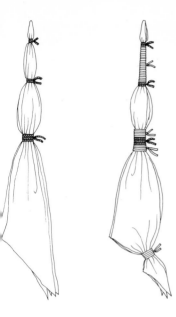

The material folded into a cone and tied.

and they can be mixed together. They are fast to sunlight and wash very well.

However they will only dye natural fibres and require highly absorbent material. Therefore use Lissapol D before dyeing. The dye must be used the moment it has been mixed or the cloth will not dye. After dyeing rinse very thoroughly a number of times.

Clean pans and other equipment with scouring powder or a bleach. Keep these pans exclusively for dyeing.

Dyeing with two dyes

A square of white batiste is folded into a cone and tied in three places. It is put into a bath of lukewarm water for about 10 minutes, then lightly squeezed and put into a green dye bath. Boil for about 15 minutes, rinse and squeeze gently. If you wish to add another colour, do a second set of bindings as in the illustration, and boil the material again for 15 minutes in a blue dye bath. Rinse and carefully remove all the pieces of string. Pull the knot so that you can cut the string without touching the material. Rinse again and spread the scarf out to dry. After 24 hours, boil in soapy water. The finished pattern will now appear as white and green circles on a blue-green background.

The drawing on the left shows the ties before the first dyeing; on the right extra ties are added before the second dyeing.

Dyeing with vat dyes

In old Javanese batik art, plant dyes were used. These plant dyes gave very beautiful colours, but the method was a troublesome one. Nowadays, even in Java, so-called vat dyes are used instead. These are fade-proof and will stand up extremely well to washing and boiling and general wear and tear to a maximum degree.

Vat dyes are in themselves insoluble in water, but when certain chemicals are added to the dye and water a chemical reaction takes place enabling the dye to dissolve and penetrate the fibres of the material.

During dyeing all batik colours look grey or brown, and it is only from the scum that one can get any inkling of the actual colour. As soon as the material is taken out of the dye bath it is oxygenated from contact with the air and begins to assume its real colour. This oxygenation continues for anything from a few minutes to an hour, depending on the dye used.

It is exciting to watch the colours change, for they run through the spectrum until they stop at last at the particular shade one has chosen for the dyeing. This can give one ideas of new colour combinations.

The process of oxygenation can be speeded up by adding sodium perborate, but this should only be used if it is absolutely necessary to see the colour of the dyed material quickly.

Preparing the dye bath

You will need:

Plastic covering	*A plastic carton*
A plastic bucket and/or bowl	*A thermometer*
A 2 pint (1 litre) measure	*Caustic soda*
Rubber gloves	*Sodium hydrosulphite*
An apron	*Cooking salt*
Indicator papers	*Dye powder*
Letter weight	*Strainer, and a piece of nylon stocking*
Stopwatch (kitchen clock)	*Newspapers*

Cover the worktable with plastic to protect it from the corrosive chemicals. Weigh the material, place it in the preliminary bath, and prepare the dye bath.

The quantity of dye required per 2 pints (1 litre) of the dye bath will be stated on the dye packet or the manufacturer's dye tables.

The easiest way to weigh the powder is on a letter weight in a plastic carton. Remember to deduct the weight of the carton!

Dissolve the dye in the plastic container by stirring in a couple of dessertspoons of the water that has been measured out for the dye bath. This must be at a temperature of 55°C. (An exception to this rule is all makes of the "cyclamen" shade, which must be dissolved in boiling water and left to stand or "vat" for 10 minutes before being added to the bath.)

The water for the bath might be called the "bearing material" for the dyeing process, so one must make quite sure that the chemicals are completely dissolved – this will only take place at the above-mentioned 55°C. If this temperature is not reached, there may be blotches on the material.

It is not necessary to test with a thermometer. A temperature of 55°C can be obtained by mixing equal quantities of boiling water and cold water. If you use water from the hot tap, you must use a thermometer.

Add the chemicals to the water, *first the caustic soda* and then the sodium hydrosulphite.

Add the chemicals to the water and never the other way round, as they might boil up and there would be a danger of getting burns on your hands and face.

Normally about $\frac{1}{28}$oz (1 g) of each of the two substances should be added to each litre of water. The measurement need not be absolutely exact and a heaped teaspoonful could quite well be used. Some makes of dye require a different quantity of sodium hydrosulphite, so it is important to read the instructions given with the dye.

The chemicals must be sealed immediately after use. If the hydrosulphite is only used occasionally the lid should be fixed down with an adhesive strip to keep it airtight, otherwise it may become unusable as the active ingredients deteriorate.

Stir the bath of water containing the two chemicals carefully with a plastic spoon, and finally add the dye solution, straining it through a hair sieve with a piece of moistened nylon stocking laid over the top. Pour water from the dye bath through the sieve until all the dye has gone through.

Leave the dye bath to stand for about 10 minutes covered with a newspaper. Meantime fill two buckets with cold water ready for rinsing the material, and any utensils used. It is also a help to keep a small plastic bowl ready to put the sieve and spoons into immediately after use.

After about 10 minutes add *cooking salt* to the water. The salt should be dissolved in a small quantity of warm water before adding it, otherwise it might make spots on the material.

There are some colours in the various makes of batik dyes for which salt should *not* be added, and also a few require double the quantity of chemicals, but for this consult the instructions given with the various brands. As a general rule it may be said that reddish-violet, indigo and black should *not* have salt added.

To make quite sure that there are no undissolved grains of dye in the bath, put on a rubber glove and run your hand over the bottom and edges of the bath before putting in the material.

Dyeing

The normal time taken for dyeing is 8 minutes, but the time may be varied depending on whether you want a lighter or a darker shade. Do not shorten or lengthen the time by more than 5 minutes or the colour will look faded.

Take the material out of the preliminary bath, carefully press out the water and place it quickly in the dye bath. Remember to use rubber gloves. The material must be submerged all the time and kept constantly in motion, using both hands to squeeze the dye into the folds. If pegs have been used, be careful not to shift their position or knock them off.

During the dyeing the strength of the dye will gradually decrease, partly because the grains of dye are absorbed by the material, and partly because the hydrosulphite is evaporating all the time. This can be countered by adding more hydrosulphite, but it is only necessary when the dyeing is to last for more than 8–10 minutes.

The strength of the dye can be tested by means of Caledon

Yellow G.N. indicator paper. The paper is dipped into the bath for a moment, and if it does not immediately turn blue, the dye is not strong enough.

Lift the material out and add half a rounded teaspoonful of sodium hydrosulphite per 2 pints (1 litre) of dye bath. Stir it in before dropping the material in again. This must all be done quickly.

If, after being in use for some time, the dye bath begins to smell sour and look muddy, this is a sign that the caustic soda has been used up. You can then add more caustic soda in the same way as the hydrosulphite (half a rounded teaspoonful per 2 pints (1 litre) of bath).

When the material is dyed, take it out and hold it for a moment over the bath so that most of the liquid runs off, before putting it into the cold rinsing water.

Change the water a couple of times.

Squeeze the material very lightly or lay it down for the water to run off, either on a table or on the floor on spread-out newspapers. The resist materials can be removed after 15 minutes.

If only one dyeing is required the work is ready to hang out to dry after a last rinsing. Add a cup of household vinegar per 2 pints (1 litre) to the last rinsing water.

After the dyeing all the articles used should be washed with plenty of soap. Remember also to wash any pegs, pieces of rubber and rubber gloves, as they may leave dye marks the next time they are used.

String is not worth using a second time.

After-treatment

The day after the dyeing, or *at the earliest* 2–3 hours after, boil out the batik articles. This can be done in soap flakes, using 1 dessertspoonful to each 2 pints (1 litre) of water.

You can buy a preparation to use for boiling out – Lissapol N – which improves the colour fastness by binding any grains of dye that are still "free". This also obviates the need for using soap flakes, which of course form a scum-like deposit in hard water.

If, however, you prefer to use soap flakes, you should use a water-softener (Calgon) at the same time, which prevents the scum penetrating the fibres of the material and forming a chalky deposit.

When the material is dry after boiling and rinsing, it can be treated like any other material of the same kind as regards ironing or pressing between hot rollers.

Practical advice

Grains of dye in the bath
If in spite of everything there are grains of dye in the bath, remove the material and quickly add 2 pints (1 litre) of boiling water and

one rounded teaspoonful of hydrosulphite. Stir this in with your hand, and the bath will be "saved".

Large baths
For large baths it is best to begin with only half the quantity of water but the full measure of chemicals and dye. After the bath has stood for 10 minutes add the remaining quantity of water.

Dye samples and notes
In addition to your usual notes and samples, it is helpful to note how dye affects different kinds of material. Cut equal-sized samples from various fabrics, and tie them loosely together so that they dye for the same length of time. It is also useful to keep samples of work that went wrong.

Keeping a dye bath for later use
A dye bath in which the colour pigments have not been used up can be kept for several hours, provided the bath is carefully covered with newspapers. If it is bottled, it can be kept for 1 to 3 weeks. If the colour pigments have been used up the dye will be weak, even after a fresh addition of hydrosulphite and caustic soda.

When the dye is to be used again, heat it to a temperature of 55°C, test with indicator paper and add chemicals as required. Let it stand for 10 minutes before using it.

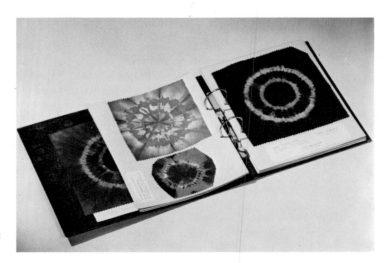

Sample folder with the samples in it.

In batik work – not least for articles of clothing – the placing of patterns and motifs on the material is very important for the final result.

Examples of folding and tying using a single dye bath

On the following pages are photographs of finished pieces of work which were dyed in a single dye bath.

Once you feel at home with the dyeing process, you can experiment and discover a wealth of possibilities for varying the combination of colours.

The drawings that accompany most of the photographs show how to fold and in some cases how to tie the material. The tying is not always included, because the reader should not feel bound to copy the finished examples shown. These are intended simply as a basis from which to work.

Once you have tried experimenting with folding material, you will soon get a feeling for it. When you have folded and tied a piece

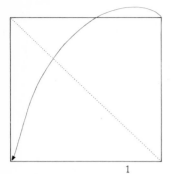

1

of work, it is a good idea to undo it and start again, so that you grasp the connection between the folding and tying and the finished result.

The knowledge that you acquire in this way will enable you to think up other ways of folding and tying. It is only when you no longer use instructions that tie-dye batik becomes really interesting. But obviously you have to gain experience first.

You will find it a help, when you want to experiment with your own ways of folding, to use a piece of paper instead of material. When you open it out again, you will be able to see the effect of the folds on the material.

Square pieces of material

Ray pattern

This is a method of folding that has been used from ancient times in many different countries. The photograph shows a scarf in three stages: folded and tied before dyeing; after a single dye bath (on the left); and a final effect where the scarf was untied and then dipped again for a few minutes in the same dye bath.

Star pattern

The material is folded first into a cone (see page 25). Then fold the material along the three dotted lines as illustrated here. Do this by taking the top point and making a fold at right-angles to the side, pressing it in sharply with the fingers and easing it out again.

Repeat this as many times as you wish, or as you find it possible to fold the material!

In the drawing the material has been folded three times. This will make a spiral. Bind the folds tightly with string without letting go of the work.

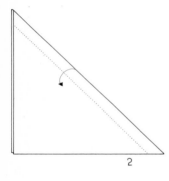

3

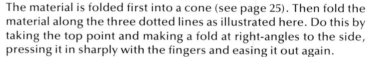

2

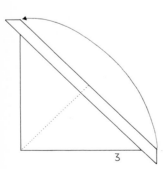

4

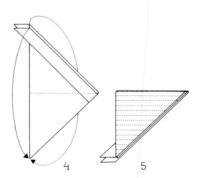

5

The ray pattern.

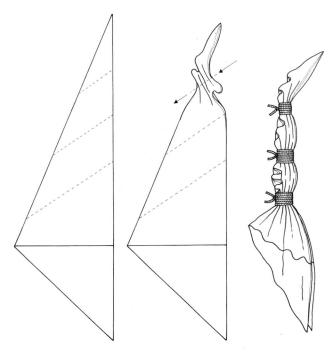

Folding and tying for the star pattern.

Corner of cloth with star pattern.

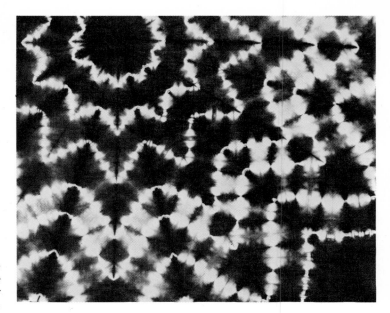

Fold the material into a double triangle (1). Then make a wide fold at the top (2). Continue by following drawings 3, 4, 5 and 6. The folds are similar to those for making a cone.

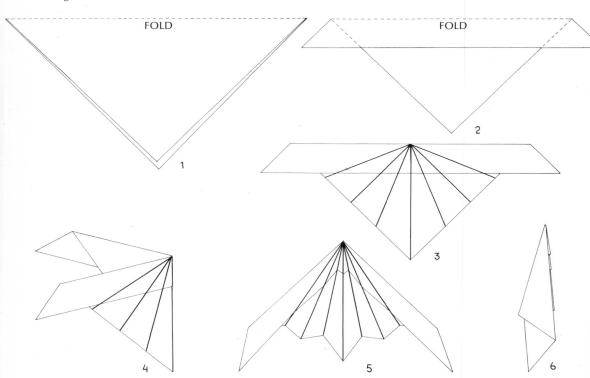

FOLD

FOLD

1

2

3

4

5

6

Paper pattern for the hat in the
photograph on this page.

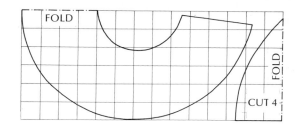

Beach frock of thin batiste – see paper pattern and
sketch of folding.

Dress and hat in satin, folded in the ray pattern and
with edge dipping (for this see page 34).

Child's frock.

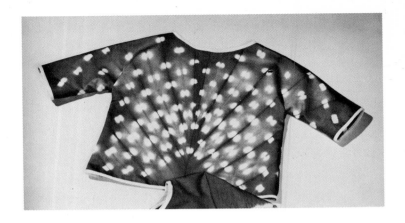

The next piece of work is an example of how to tie-dye children's frocks cut out to a paper pattern. The first is bound with string with the deepest folds at the bottom. The second has pieces of rubber fastened on with clothes pegs, and the pleats are deepest at the top. Each dress is cut out before tying and dyeing.

Fold the front and back separately. Make a crease down each centre line and fold each side separately so that the pleats are even. Smooth the folds with your thumbnail, and then iron. You must be extremely accurate, or the result will be slipshod.

The dye bath should be a 4 pint (2 litre) bath, which is about the minimum for obtaining good results.

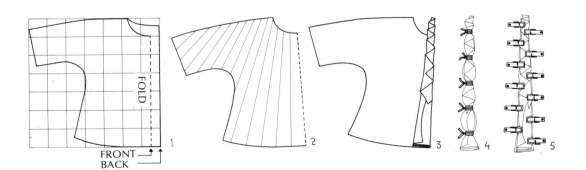

Working with colour

For beginners it is safest to use one dye. One dye will produce shades of the same colour. Keep to this one-tone principle to create subtle effects before proceeding to use related colours. Avoid using contrasting colours until you understand thoroughly how they work.

If you do not feel certain of your colour sense, work from the basic principles of colour which are quite simple to follow. The illustration shows the colours arranged in a circular colour chart. The primary colours – red, blue and yellow – cannot be produced by mixing. These colours can, however, be mixed with each other. Red and yellow make orange. If there is more red than yellow, the result will be a reddish-orange. If there is more yellow, you will get an orange-yellow. In the same way, red and blue make violet.

You can go on mixing colours that fall side by side and expanding the colour chart in this way. Related colours can always be used together.

Complementary or contrasting colours, such as red and green, must be treated with more caution as they are inclined to "fight" with one another.

Working in a number of colours can give very attractive results, but you need to be fairly sure about blending colours together harmoniously. (See Colour Tables in Appendix.)

The colour chart showing colour combinations. Green is often regarded as a primary colour, because you cannot obtain a pure green by mixing blue and yellow.

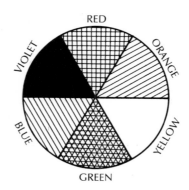

Dyeing for effect, and multi-coloured batik

Effectively used, a streak of colour on a monochrome background can be dramatic and exciting. To create this effect with tie-dye, dip small areas of a piece of material briefly in a dye bath. This bath is prepared by using the same quantities of dye powder and chemicals for a 2 pint (1 litre) bath, but using only a ½ pint (¼ litre) of water. The dye is so strong that the material is normally only dipped for 45 seconds. The time varies from 15 to 70 seconds depending on the colour depth desired. At places where it is not possible to dip the material, dye can be sprayed into folds and pleats with an ear syringe. After effect dyeing, the dye bath can be made up to a normal 2 pint (1 litre) basic bath by adding 1½ pints (¾ litre) of water.

The following diagrams and illustrations show different examples of effect dyeing.

Scarf with its edge dipped.

Method of folding and dipping the above four-cornered scarf.

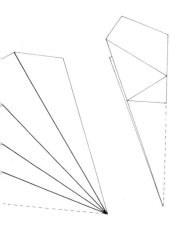

1

2

Rectangular cloth. 1. the material folded; 2. and tied; 3. immersed in the basic bath; 4. the middle tie removed; 5. dipped in the effect bath; 6. the finished cloth with all ties removed.

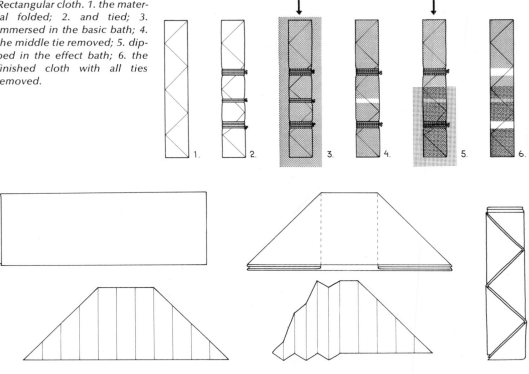

1.   2.   3.   4.   5.   6.

This shows the finished work and a demonstration of folding and tying. The pegs are used to hold the pleats in position during tying.

Preparing a table mat for dyeing.

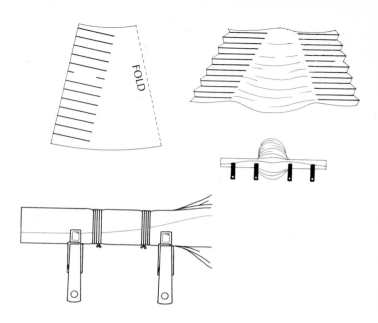

FOLD

A photograph of the finished mat and the tied mat folded ready for dyeing. The pegs have cycle-tyre rubber underneath.

Scarf in thin batiste, dyed in a basic bath. The material is rolled tightly round a matchstick. It is then gathered together and bound round with a thin linen thread. The tips of the bound parts are dipped in an effect bath for 25 seconds. See diagrams 1–4.

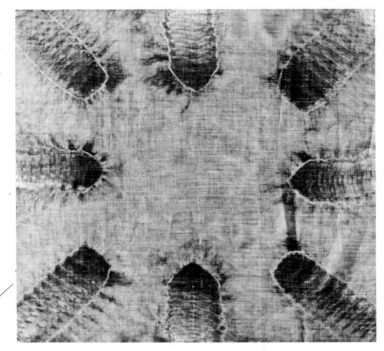

Below:

Stole with edging. The material is folded into a cone. The whole of the material with the sharply marked folds is dipped in a basic bath for 8 minutes, rinsed, and most of the water pressed out between newspapers. The material, still in a cone shape, is now folded four times along one edge and not more than ⅜ in (1 cm) is dipped in the effect bath, the rest being held firmly in both hands. Rinse out and fold the edge on the other side, dipping and rinsing in the same way. Press out the moisture, and dry and iron the material. Fold it again in the opposite direction, and repeat the whole process.

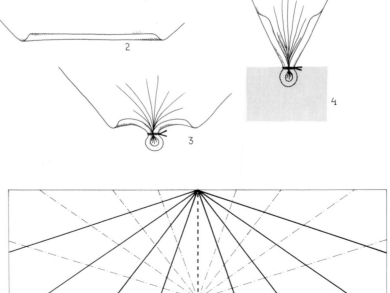

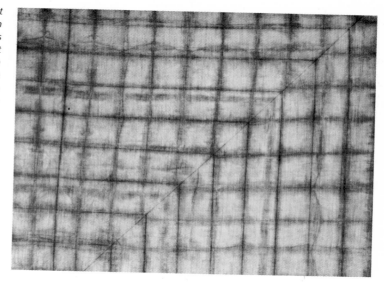

Part of a batiste scarf. It was first folded into accordion pleats in one direction, and the edges dipped in an effect bath. Then it was folded in the same way in the other direction, and the edges dipped in a different colour. This gives a check pattern in two colours.

Winding a piece of folded material round a bottle before dipping the edge in an effect bath prevents sharp folds.

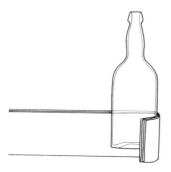

Addition of "blind dye" to an effect bath

If you have a light background, a dark effect might upset the colour harmony. If you wish the effect to be paler than can be achieved by dipping the material for the shortest possible time, use a so-called *blind dye* instead. This is a solution of warm water and chemicals *without* dye powder. Add 1 heaped teaspoonful of caustic soda and 1 heaped teaspoonful of sodium hydrosulphite per 2 pints (1 litre) of water. To a ½ pint (¼ litre) effect bath add only ¾ litre blind dye. Pour the effect bath and the blind dye in together, and test the colour with indicator paper or a small strip of the material.

Bleaching

Apart from being used to lighten a dye bath, a blind dye can sometimes save a piece of blotchy work.

After moistening the material thoroughly in lukewarm water, soak it in the blind dye for 30 minutes, moving it constantly.

Note! The light parts will be slightly dyed unless they are isolated again, because the dye that is dissolved by the blind dye will be deposited on these portions.

Working without ties

Sometimes you may wish to work spontaneously to create uninhibited designs. It is possible to use your hands as the isolating material. This produces exciting, immediate results but obviously the method has its limitations.

As an example of such spontaneous work we will run through the stages of production of the table runner shown in the illustration, to give you an idea of how you can literally create with your hands.

You will need:
A piece of material 16 × 30 in (40 × 75 cm)
4 effect baths in wide shallow bowls. (The quantity of dye is small and there must be room for your hands)
4 bowls of rinsing water

Wet the material with lukewarm water and fold it in half along the short side. Then take hold of the centre of the fold with one hand and gather the material together with the other, holding it tightly about 6 in (15 cm) from the point. Still holding it tightly with one hand, dip the point of the material into effect bath No. 1, working the dye into the material with the other hand. Dye for 60 seconds. Without loosening your grip on the material, rinse the dyed part in cold water.

Stages in dyeing a table runner without using any ties.

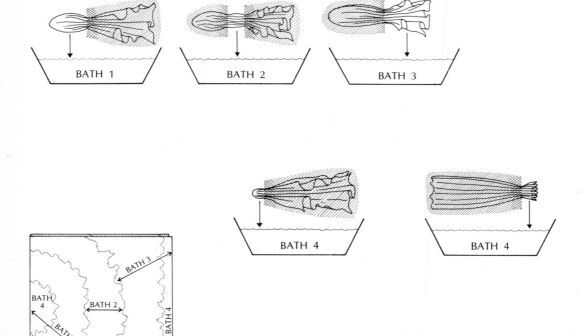

40

Then hold the dyed part firmly in your left hand and grip tightly with the right hand about 2½ in (6–7 cm) further along. Dip this narrow strip into dye bath No. 2, keeping the rest of the material well away from the dye. Twist the material to ensure that it is thoroughly wetted by the relatively small bath, at the same time pressing the hands together to work the colour well into the folds. Dye for 60 seconds. Rinse the work without loosening your grip.

Next hold the material firmly covering the piece last dyed, and dip the bottom ends into dye bath No. 3. Dye for 60 seconds. Work the dye into the material with your free hand. Rinse.

Still retaining the centre fold, open the material out. Take hold of it again in the middle of the fold with one hand, while gathering it together with the other. Dip about 2 in (4–5 cm) at the very tip into dye bath No. 4, taking care that the rest of the material does not come in contact with the bath. Dye for 60 seconds. Rinse.

Open the material right out, fold in half along the long side, and in one hand gather the two short sides into small folds, leaving 1½ in (3–4 cm) free. Dip these edges into the same dye bath as before, No. 4. Take care to work the dye well into the short folds. Dye for 60 seconds. Rinse without loosening your hold. Open the material right out, rinse and proceed as usual.

If you wish to dye a lining to the table runner in one of the colours used, turn that particular effect bath into an ordinary dye bath.

Working spontaneously like this can produce all sorts of fascinating effects.

Even tiny areas can be dyed if you can have an assistant to pour or spray the dye while you hold the folds tightly.

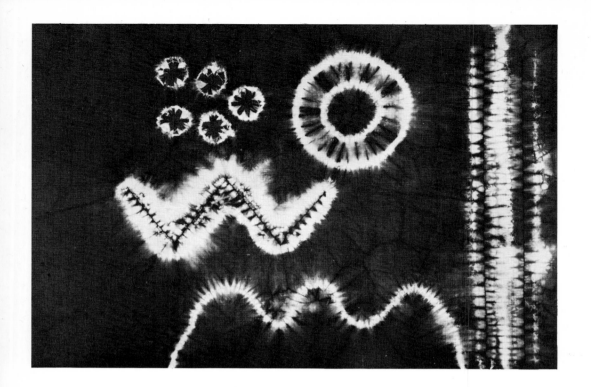

Sample of material with various tritik tackings.

Tritik

Tritik is a technique of producing a particular pattern effect by stitching with needle and thread. The finished tritik pattern will consist of rows of dots or short broken lines. First draw the pattern on the back of the material to form guide lines for the subsequent tacking. Use strong, white linen thread for tacking, but remember that the needle and thread must not be too coarse, or they may leave permanent marks on the material.

Start with a secure knot and tack as evenly as possible until the whole pattern is tacked. Always end on the same side as you started on, leaving the thread hanging.

Change to a fresh thread at all sharp corners, and where there is a break in the pattern. Straight lines, narrow zigzag lines and curved lines can be tacked without changing thread. These are all recommended for a beginner. (See drawings 1–4.)

When the tacking is finished, draw the threads up tightly and tie them together without allowing the gathers to slacken.

The tritik work is now ready for dyeing. Use the lightest colour first. When the material is dry, work further tackings. The material can be dyed again before removing the first tackings.

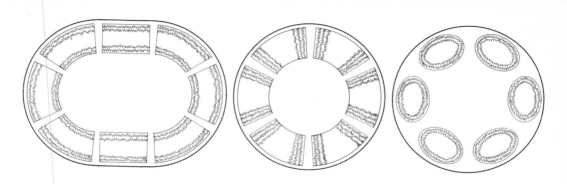

Suggestions for tackings on rounded articles.

For large pieces of tritik work a sewing machine is useful. Use a strong buttonhole twist, so that the thread will not break when it is drawn up and tied. Set the machine for large stitches.

Illustrations of tritik methods and variations

Zig-zag tacking for tritik.

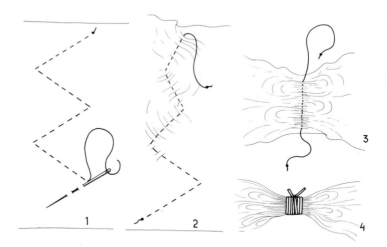

A zig-zag line
Tack as shown in drawing 1. Draw the gathers tightly and evenly as in drawings 2 and 3. Tie the loose ends together. The area can be further tied with string.

The result resembles that obtained with a simple tie, but has recognizable differences.

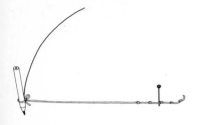

"Compass" of pencil, string and pin.

A circle

More accurate circles can be achieved by the tritik technique than by tying. It is essential to have a guide line. An easy way of drawing circles, using a piece of string, a pencil and a pin, is shown in the illustration.

Parallel lines or double tritik

Parallel lines can be made by tacking a tuck in the material. Fold the material along one or more marked lines, pressing the creases flat with the thumb. Work the running stitches as shown in the drawing. Draw the threads up very tightly and tie them round before dyeing.

   This method may be developed into multiple tritik by tacking together several layers of material. After drawing up the threads the isolation can be strengthened by tying string tightly round the material. Alternatively tie loosely between the gathers for a different effect.

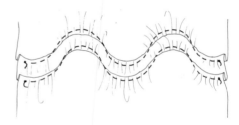

Double tritik.

Multiple tritik.

Tritik with loose ties between the gathered rows of tacking.

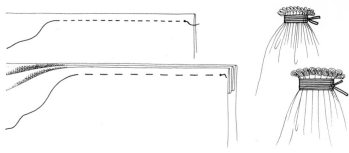

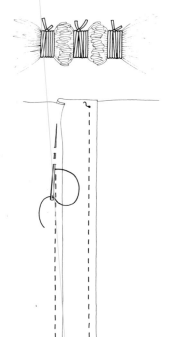

Combination of tie-dye batik and tritik
Batik work can combine several techniques. For example you can fold the material as in tie-dye batik, but isolate your design with tritik.

In the illustration below a Greek-key pattern is stitched through several layers of batiste. To ensure that the pattern will emerge consistently the needle must always be inserted vertically from above and below.

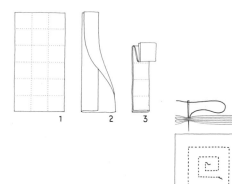

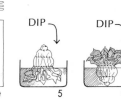

Folding and tacking through several layers of material, and dipping in an effect bath.

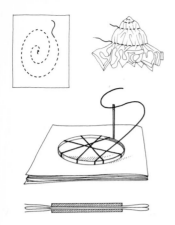

Isolation with a plastic lid

Fold a piece of material 18 × 24 in (45 × 60 cm) three times lengthwise and four times across, to form a square. Sew a plastic lid on each side of the folded material, in the centre of the square. The lids must be of equal size. Attach them by inserting the needle close to the edge of the lid and working backwards and forwards drawing the thread tight. The pattern emerges as twelve white circles which could be used as a basis for block printing. The shape can be varied by using stiff cardboard etc.

Using a plastic lid for isolating.

Knotting objects in

Various objects (such as uncoloured wooden beads, glass beads, buttons, dried peas and pieces of cork) may be tied or stitched firmly into the material. Bear in mind that it is not the article enclosed that gives the isolation, but only the string or thread tied round it. The isolation achieved therefore takes the form of a ring, the size and shape of which will depend on the article tied inside. This method of isolation is particularly useful if you are working on a pattern containing small details.

BEADS

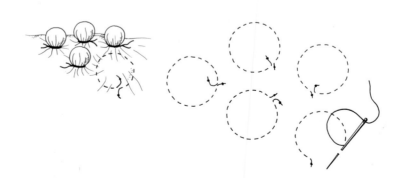

Isolating with beads.

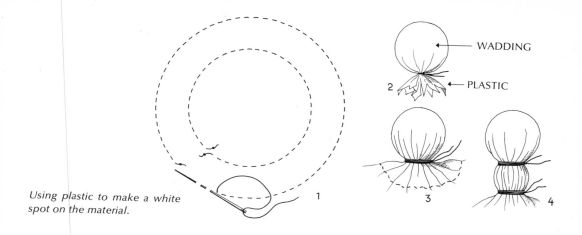

WADDING

2 ← PLASTIC

1

3

4

Using plastic to make a white spot on the material.

How to make a white spot on the material
If you want to make a white spot on the material, you can cover whatever you have tied in with plastic, which must be secured with thread or string. Plastic may also be used as a covering when there is no object underneath. These isolated patches can be decorated in various ways with wax batik or block printing.

Tunic with tritik

You will need:
About 2¼ yards (2 m) of material
8 pint (4 litre) bath
6 pint (3 litre) bath
½ pint (¼ litre) effect bath, in the same colour as the 8 pint (4 litre) bath
String, linen thread, newspapers

When you have cut out the tunic, draw the pattern on the wrong side as shown in the drawing at the top of page 48.
Sew along the pencil lines with even running stitches, using fine white linen thread. The drawing must be absolutely identical on front and back, so that the coloured areas meet exactly on the shoulder seam when the work is made up.

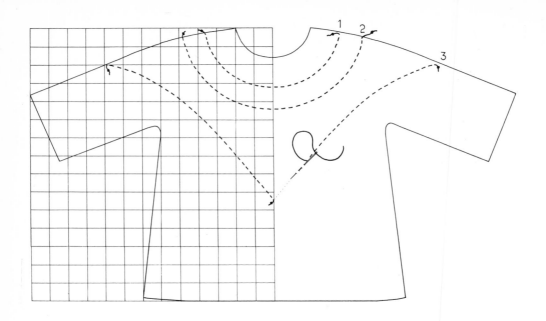

STRING

1

2

3

4

4 STRING

Paper pattern, tacking and gathering of the tunic. The drawing on the right shows the tacking and gathering of the collar.

Take care that the threads running down from the shoulder seam to the centre of the tunic meet on the centre line. When all the lines have been tacked, draw the threads up tightly and fasten off. So that the ties will be exactly the same, bind them with pieces of string cut to the same length.

Dye the lower part of the tunic first in the large bath. It is advisable to protect the upper part with a piece of plastic. Rinse twice in cold water. Cover the dyed part with a plastic bag. Dye the top part of the tunic and the two pieces of material for facing and collar in the 6 pint (3 litre) bath, and rinse well.

Remove the tying string and tacking threads from the collar and uppermost row on the neck (see No. 1 on the diagram). Gather the work together with your fingers just below the second line of tacking, holding the folds tightly in your left hand while you dip it into the effect bath for 35 seconds. Fold the collar and dip the short piece above the gathering in the same way. Rinse the work well and spread it out on a thick layer of newspapers to oxidize and dry.

Wax batik

To many people wax batik is "proper" batik. It is an art form that has reached fantastic artistic heights. But the fact that it is a skilled technique which has been used by textile artists from the Pacific Islands to India and Europe does not mean that one cannot experiment with this exciting medium as an amateur.

A scarf that has been given a checked effect by an easy method. The vertical and horizontal stripes are painted on with a broad brush dipped in fluid wax.

The knowledge and experience gained from working with tie-dye batik will stand you in good stead with the rather more demanding wax batik. At the same time you must realize that working with wax is a slower process than those previously described, but in compensation this method allows far greater freedom of expression.

You do not need any great talent as a painter to be able to work in wax batik, as you can go a long way with the simple geometric forms. In batik work it is often more a question of colours and their distribution on the material that is decisive, rather than the actual pattern. We will start with the easiest form, in which the wax is applied with a brush, and then discuss the use of the traditional tjanting.

Round bristle brush.

Flat bristle brush.

Wax batik with a brush

You will need:
Material (cotton, wool mixtures, cotton velvet)
Wax
Brushes
An electric plate
An enamelled pan
A thermometer that can measure up to 200°C
Steel wire
Pieces of rag
Newspaper, iron, white spirit

A radiator bristle brush with the handle cut down.

A brush with the bristles cut to give a striped or checked pattern.

Materials and patterns
All cotton materials which are not too thick and have been washed free of dressing are suitable. Dye soon wears off synthetic material because it does not penetrate the fibres, but is deposited on the surface of the material.

To begin with, prepare simple geometric patterns that only need to be dipped into one bath. You can always elaborate later if you wish.

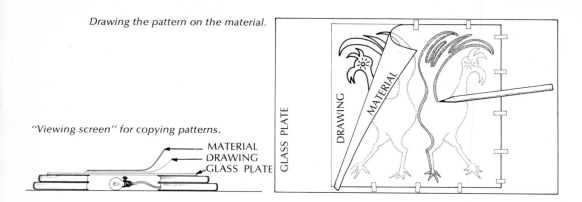

Drawing the pattern on the material.

"Viewing screen" for copying patterns.

MATERIAL
DRAWING
GLASS PLATE

GLASS PLATE

DRAWING

MATERIAL

There are various ways of transferring designs to material. The simplest method of enlarging a pattern is to draw the sketch on squared paper, and then fold the material into the corresponding number of squares (these squares will of course be larger than on the paper). Now copy the pattern freehand onto the grid of larger squares on the material.

Carbon paper should not be used. If you have a glass plate with an electric light underneath, you can lay first the pattern and then the material on the glass, and you will then be able to see the design clearly. Trace with a soft pencil or drawing charcoal.

Combinations of and elaborations upon basic geometric shapes, arranged symmetrically and combined to form a cohesive whole and used on a tapa, or loin cloth.

Preparing for waxing

Cover the work table with a sheet of plastic, and then a newspaper to catch any drips. A piece of foam rubber makes a good underlay.

It is advisable to stretch the material on a frame, either bought or improvised. Attach it to the frame with fine pins. Small pieces of work may be laid directly on the covered table. Lift the material as you wax, to prevent it sticking to the newspaper.

An example of wax batik. The "marbled" effect is produced by carefully crushing the material in a tub of cold water.

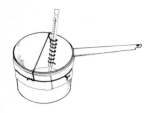

Pan for wax.

Wax

There are several different kinds of ready-mixed wax available. Pure *beeswax* is rarely used for batik because people generally prefer patterns with cracking, and pure beeswax is so pliant that it does not crack easily. The ready-mixed brands have substances added to ensure an even crackle effect. If you want a very marked effect add *paraffin*. The addition of pure wax will result in thin crackle lines.

Ordinary white paraffin wax can be used. (See section on this on page 78.) Use a small enamelled pan for heating up the wax. Wax must never be heated over an open fire or a spirit stove – electric heating should always be used. A safe and convenient method is to work with a single hot plate covered with a large asbestos sheet, and to place your pan on this. The asbestos will prevent the wax from getting too hot too quickly – you can lift the pan off the heat when the wax shows signs of getting too hot.

Wipe the brush on a piece of steel wire or a strip of netting stretched across the pan. This prevents inflammable wax running down the outside of the pan. As an extra precaution, bind a strip of rag round the top of the pan to catch the drips. Balance the brush on the wire to keep it warm and soft while working on the waxing.

As shown in the drawing a thermometer is fitted to the pan to measure the temperature of the wax. It is held in a wire spiral. Heat the wax slowly and maintain between 130–150°C. It is very important to use a thermometer, as there is a danger of the wax catching fire if the temperature exceeds 170°C.

If the temperature approaches this level, the wax will start smoking violently and the fluid constituents in it will evaporate. It will then lose its usefulness for batik.

If the wax should catch fire, *never* use water to put it out. Place a lid or a thick layer of wet newspapers over the pan.

If the temperature does not get higher than 120°C the wax will be deposited as a thick white layer over the material without penetrating the fibres, and it will peel off in the subsequent dye bath.

Sketch of a scarf waxed with a cut-out brush to give a striped pattern.

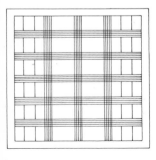

Waxing

It is wise to start applying the wax with a pointed brush. Practice with this gives a good grounding. When you feel confident, experiment with brushes of different types and sizes.

Always saturate new brushes with hot wax before use.

Using a cut-out brush.

Suggestions for striped patterns.

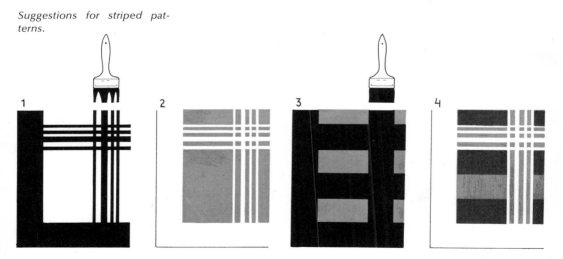

The wax must penetrate the fibres of the material to be isolated, without actually running through. Check that you have waxed evenly by holding the material at a slant. The waxed areas should look quite smooth on the front and the back.

When using a number of dye baths, check the waxed parts regularly. Any places where the wax is damaged will have to be repaired by re-applying wax to the back of the material when it is dry.

When applying the wax you can choose between colouring the pattern or colouring the background. If you choose the first method, leave the pattern uncovered and apply the wax *round* the material. If you choose the second method, it is the pattern that must be covered with wax. The method you choose depends on the final colour effect you wish to achieve.

Cracking

This marbling effect on the material occurs when the dye penetrates fine cracks in the wax. These cracks are produced by carefully crushing the material – either at random, leaving the effect to chance, or by breaking the wax at previously determined places. Fine or coarse cracks can be obtained by mixing two types of wax. (See page 54.)

At ordinary room temperature the wax is so malleable after being applied that it is difficult to crack. It must therefore be cooled down by placing it in a good-sized bath of cold water. The bath has to be fairly large to avoid crumpling the material, because you may not want cracking over the whole of the work. Crush the material only at the places where you wish the cracking to appear.

Symmetrical patterns

Symmetrical and mirror patterns can be made on thin materials by folding the material in half and allowing the wax to penetrate both layers.

Cracking must be done on the folded material, as the layers cannot be separated until dyeing has been completed and the wax removed.

This shows how to work over the waxed layer with your fingers to make it crack. This should be done under water, but is demonstrated here "dry" for technical photographic reasons.

Dyeing

The equipment and procedure for dyeing are the same as for tie-dye batik, with one exception. Preliminary and dye baths must be cool. It is therefore essential to use a thermometer. See that the baths do not exceed the melting temperature given with the instructions on the different kinds of wax.

Dyes which normally take effect at higher temperatures can be used in a cool dye bath if you lengthen the dyeing time.

When you are working in a number of colours, wax is applied several times, the idea being that the wax must cover colours that are to remain unchanged. Waxing must always be done on completely dry material.

It is essential to think out your colour blends carefully. Begin dyeing with the light colour, and leave the cracking for the last and darkest.

After-treatment

After several rinses the material may be squeezed, since the wax has fulfilled its function as an isolating agent. The wax must now be removed.

The simplest and most effective method is to iron the material between newspapers. The iron should not be too hot. Keep changing the newspapers all the time. Printer's ink has a nasty habit of coming off. Blotting paper or blank news-sheet is ideal.

After ironing, the dark edges that will inevitably appear in or round the pattern can be removed if the material is washed in white spirit. Then boil for 10 minutes in soapy water.

Another method of removing the wax is to scrape off as much as you can with the blunt edge of a knife, and to boil the material in plenty of water for about 10 minutes. Add a dessertspoonful of soap flakes and a teaspoonful of soda ash per 2 pints (1 litre) of water. Remove any wax which floats to the surface. Rinse immediately several times in hot water. If there is still wax on the material when it is dry, you can iron it between several layers of newspaper. Wash off the dark edges in white spirit. The work may need another boiling in soapy water.

Opposite:

Dress on left:
The design is waxed on to white poplin with a brush.

Dress on right:
A combination of tritik and waxing to achieve a special colour effect. After the tritik pattern has been worked and dyed one colour, it is covered with wax and the dress dyed a different shade of the same colour. The pattern emerges as a light shade on a darker background.

Instead of boiling the material you may dip it alternately into absolutely boiling soapy water and clear, cold water. Repeat this at least five or six times. The bath in white spirit will not then be necessary. Half a teaspoon of Lissapol D can be added to the boiling water.

Working with paper patterns

Begin by drawing the wax design on the paper pattern. Your design must balance, and allow for darts and seams. In order to use the dress design to best effect, it is advisable to do the cutting out before the waxing, but this is not essential.

Combination of tritik and waxing

When combining tritik or tie-dye batik with wax batik it is advisable to boil the material between the two methods of treatment to remove the chemicals, as they discolour the material if they are not removed before ironing. Ironing is necessary, as wax should be applied only to material that is completely smooth.

The pattern is drawn with a tjanting. The material is stretched on an adjustable frame.

Working with tjanting and wax

Tjanting is the Javanese name for a small, pipelike tool used to apply wax to the material. It consists of a small copper container which holds the hot, fluid wax, and one or more spouts. The container is attached to a handle of wood or bamboo. Tjantings are obtainable in good art supply shops.

In the East Indies tjantings with as many as seven spouts have been used to draw parallel lines.

You can see from examples in museums how the Javanese artists drew stylized flowers with these tjantings. Some had spouts of different diameters, so that it was possible to draw fine outlines or use the tjanting to fill in spaces.

61

Preparation for using the tjanting

Wax must be heated to about 130°C to obtain a consistent flow. If it is hotter than this it will run too quickly, and the lines will become blurred and blotchy. Pure beeswax melts at a low temperature (60°C) and can be used to eliminate cracking.

Do not overfill the bowl of the tjanting, as the wax will cool and congeal before it is used up. Refilling the bowl allows a moment's relaxation.

The tjanting is filled by dipping it into the pan of fluid wax. It has to be held down in the wax long enough for the copper to be heated through, so that the wax does not congeal too quickly while you are working.

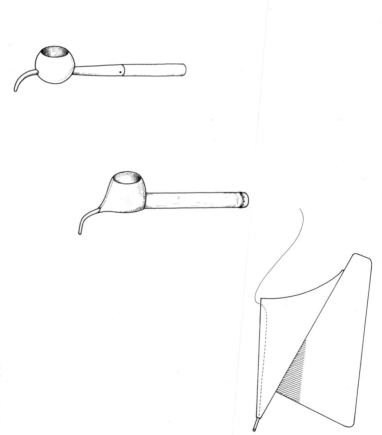

Three different tjantings. The bottom one is cone-shaped and has a wooden handle. If the shaded portion is cut away, the tjanting can be hung on the edge of a pan.

Tjantings with several spouts.

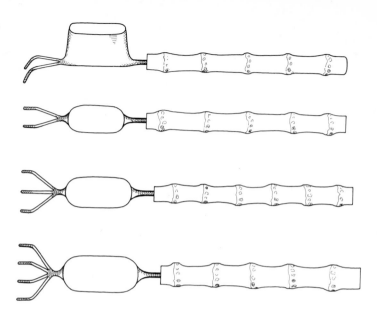

Hold a small piece of rag under the spout, so that it does not drip when you transfer the tjanting to the material.

To prevent any impurities in the wax from getting into the spout, it is advisable to fix a tiny piece of wadding at the mouth.

The small piece of wire that is shown in the bottom drawing opposite prevents the wax running through too quickly. The wire must not be thicker than a piece of sewing cotton. A single wire from an electric flex would be suitable.

Never try to clean the spout. Even with quite a fine wire there is a danger of making the opening larger and uneven, so that the tjanting would have to be discarded. All that is necessary is to hold the tjanting down in the pan of melted wax and any impurities that may have got into the spout will float out. If this does not work, push the impurities out through the hot spout with a single bristle from a brush.

It is not necessary to clean the tjanting after use. Simply let the wax harden, and next time you use it hold it down in the melted wax until the remains of the wax dissolve.

Simple designs executed with tjantings having two, three and four spouts respectively. Patterns arise almost of their own accord when tjantings with several spouts are used.

Fine linen, cotton, muslin and silk are ideal materials to use with a tjanting because they have a smooth surface and are not too thick. The spout must move easily over the material. Stretch very fine materials over a frame before waxing.

To prevent the wax sticking to the work surface and the material slipping about while you are working on it, use an underlay. Thin foam rubber is recommended for fine materials, and sandpaper for tougher fabrics. Glue the underlay to a wooden board. When you have finished working remove wax from the sandpaper using newspaper and a hot iron.

From sketch to material

Draw the pattern full size on paper. To give an impression of how the pattern or design will look, colour it with a brush. Transfer the pattern to the material, drawing freehand with a soft pencil or a piece of charcoal. The sketch marks will be washed away in the boiling. Brush or blow any excess charcoal dust from the material.

The pattern on the dress was drawn with a tjanting and brush on a white ground. The work was dipped in one colour.

Using the tjanting

With a little practice the tjanting is easy to control. The photograph on page 61 shows how to draw with a tjanting. The spout must be kept in contact with the material all the time and held slightly sideways, the angle depending on the type of tjanting, and what feels best for you.

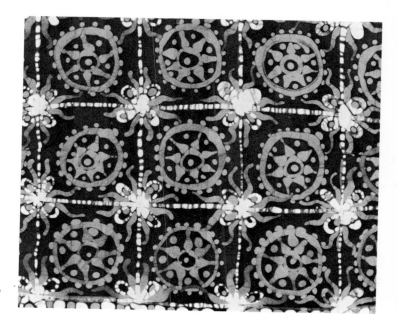

Detail of dress pattern in photograph on page 66.

Above: *Tjanting work on dress and hat. The pleated effect comes from using a striped satin.*

Left: *The tunic shows a combination of tjanting work and surface filling with a broad brush. The large surface is cracked before the dye bath.*

If you want to start by using a relatively simple method to create your own design, shake a brush full of wax over a piece of material. Then use a tjanting to join the spots of wax in spontaneous patterns. This kind of work can do a great deal to sharpen your sense of balance and form.

Wall hanging on calico. The eight large circles are drawn with a wax brush. The figures inside are also drawn with a brush. The fine lines inside the circles are drawn with a tjanting. The material is dipped in one colour and given after-treatment. Then the drawing is done with the tjanting on the dyed background, and the material dipped again, this time in the second colour.

In Java they used to hang the material vertically while decorating it. We normally wax on a horizontal surface, but if it seems more comfortable use a frame and hold it at an angle.

Use of stencils

Methods of applying wax can be combined with stencilling. Transparent or coloured self-adhesive contact material is used. The clear kind is preferable, as one can see any drawing underneath. When cutting out stencil patterns it is easiest to keep to geometrical figures. Cut out the stencils with a sharp, pointed knife, and see they are kept in one piece as any disconnected portions will fall off when the protective paper is removed.

Lay the self-adhesive contact material on the material, and apply wax with a brush through the gaps in the stencil.

Try giving your own imagination rein – the possibilities are endless.

Cutting designs in the wax
Use a knitting needle to draw a pattern on the waxed material. This is a good method for producing fine lines and monograms.

Wipe off the wax that is deposited on the point of the needle. Work carefully so as not to damage the material.

Table napkin case. Contact material was used for the stencil. The material was dyed a light yellow-brown before the pattern was waxed through the stencil. The stencil was removed, the work cracked and dyed a dark brown.

Printing block batik

Left:

Copper printing blocks in various geometric shapes may be bought ready-made.

Middle:

Printing blocks with flat-headed brass nails. First scratch the design on the block and then drive in the nails to an even height. Check this by turning the block upside down onto a flat surface. The heads of the nails must not touch each other. Use different sized heads for variation.

Right:

Two diamond shapes with brass nails. The smaller shape fits into the larger one. Use to create effects with two colours.

The term "printing block" refers to any object used to press fluid wax on to material.

A flat, shallow pan must be used. Lay a thick layer of felt on the bottom to act as an absorbent pad, and barely cover with wax. Keep at a temperature of between 130°C and 140°C. Only the printing edge of the block is dipped into the melted wax.

Before starting, the printing block must stand on the felt underlay long enough for it to become heated through. As in tjanting work, hold a small piece of rag under the printing block until you set it down on the material.

Think out in advance where the prints are to be placed. Take a number of impressions on paper or material, cut them out, and arrange them on the material you are going to print. Remember that prints carelessly made will be untidy and messy.

Printing blocks can be bought or made. For ideas see the illustrations.

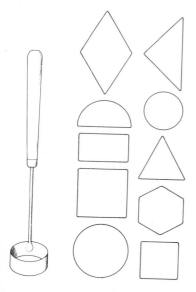

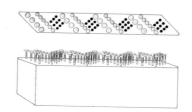

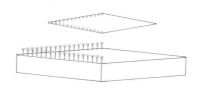

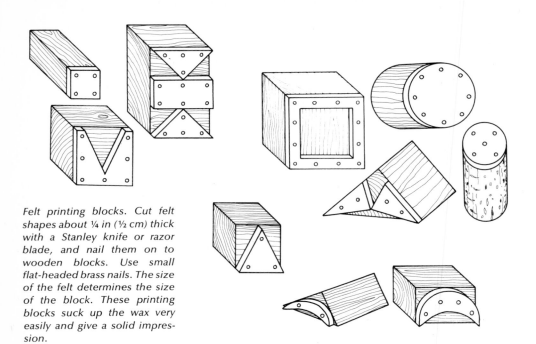

Felt printing blocks. Cut felt shapes about ¼ in (½ cm) thick with a Stanley knife or razor blade, and nail them on to wooden blocks. Use small flat-headed brass nails. The size of the felt determines the size of the block. These printing blocks suck up the wax very easily and give a solid impression.

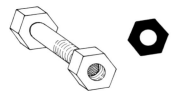

Brass bolt and nut used to produce a characteristic block shape.

The inner metal casing of a lipstick holder, fitted with a cork handle, makes small circles.

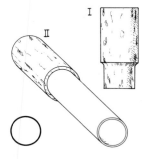

A round wooden rod bound round once with coarse linen folded in half and projecting not more than about ½ in (1 cm) beyond the end of the stick. Bind the linen and stitch the join with fine thread.

Rectangular piece of wood with coarse linen bound round it, shaped so as to make impressions in two different sizes.

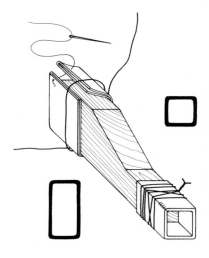

Linen printing block designed to make circular impressions. A piece of thin copper plate fixed to a wooden handle will produce lines.

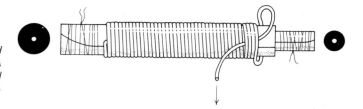

Lino-cut used on a block.

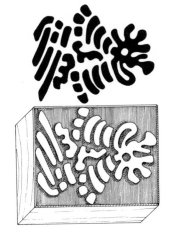

Right:
Combination of isolation with a plastic lid and a block.

Block printing over striped tie-dye pattern.

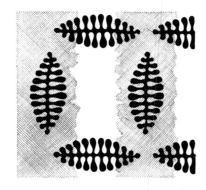

Left:
Section of a loofah. This is a fibrous plant pod imported from Korea and obtainable from large chemist's shops. Soak the loofah in water so that it swells out. Let it dry and then cut it into sections with a very sharp knife.

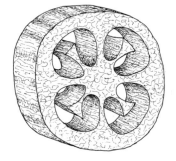

Right:
Print made by a loofah.

Bead-work and batik

A completed batik design can be decorated with embroidery or bead-work. This can be very effective.

Patterned material and batik

Particular effects can be achieved using material that already has a pattern or a stripe.

Silk batik

Special dyes are used for batik work on silk – they *cannot* however be used for cotton materials. These dyes have to be treated differently from other batik dyes. Silk batik work will not stand dry cleaning or washing in hot soapy water. Detailed instructions for use are supplied with the special dyes, but here is the main outline of the process.

Mix the dye powder with hot water. Add acetic acid of 32 per cent strength. Let it stand for 10–15 minutes and stir constantly. Cool,

Silk scarf waxed with a brush and dipped in one colour.

strain and store in labelled bottles. This dye will keep for several weeks, and can be re-used.

Before dyeing, dilute the concentrated dye with cold water, the amount depending on the depth of colour desired. Experiment by dipping small scraps of silk in the dye bath. You must rinse them in running water and dry them before you can judge the shade.

Dye for about 10–15 minutes. Rinse the material in running water and then soak for 10 minutes in a cold bath containing acetic acid (32 per cent). (Use 40 g acetic acid to each litre of water.) To prevent the dye running when using a number of colours, rinse between each dye bath in a weak solution of acetic acid. This bath should be half the strength of the one given above.

Remember that silk materials will not stand boiling, and must be rinsed in water that is not too hot.

Tritik and tie-dye batik on silk

If you want to use tritik on thin silken material, use a fine needle and sewing silk for the tacking to avoid leaving marks on the finished work. The pattern can be drawn on white tissue paper which you pin on to the material, tacking along the lines of the pattern. The tissue paper can be removed without difficulty when the tacking is finished. This same method can of course be used on cotton materials. It has the advantage that it saves drawing on the actual material.

1. Tacking through tissue paper. 2 and 3. Drawing up and tying. Isolating with fine string tied round twice, and a clothes peg with a piece of cycle tyre rubber underneath.

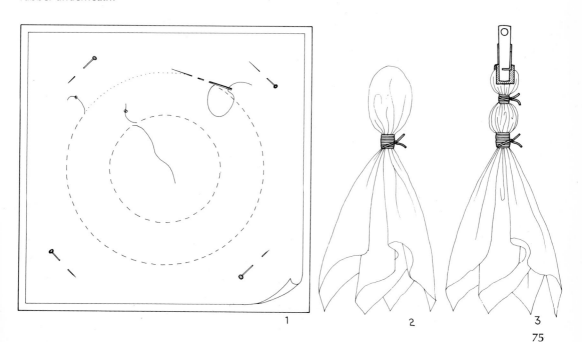

1 2 3

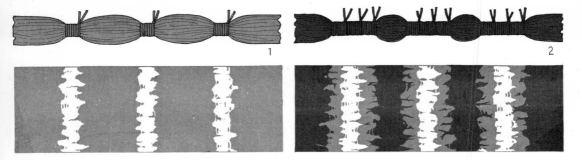

Tying for the dye bath to achieve a three-colour effect.

A scarf dipped in two dye baths.

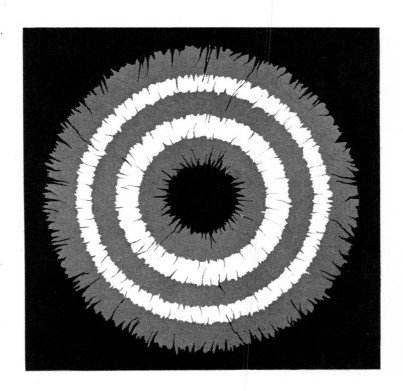

Wax batik on silk

Draw your design on the silk with a thin piece of charcoal, then stretch the silk on a frame by means of *fine* pins stuck into a strip of linen bound round the frame. Wax as usual.

Wax is easy to remove from silk. Place the material between layers of newspaper, and iron it at the correct temperature for silk. After ironing, the grease shadows must be removed by washing in pure benzine. Do not use hot soapy water. Wear a clean pair of rubber gloves as benzine will remove any residue of dye on the gloves. Make sure that the windows are open and that there are no burning gas jets or open fires in the room.

To clean silk batik work after wearing, wash in benzine. Do not dry clean.

Batik with paraffin wax

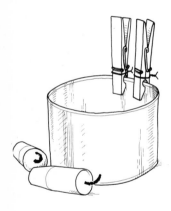

Bag with paraffin wax resist on heavy linen. The paraffin wax is applied to both sides of the material, as it is difficult to get it to penetrate. The material is dyed once.

This can be bought, or melted down from old candles with the wicks removed. It gives a very clear impression on thin materials with a smooth surface; on rough fabrics the results are coarser.

One of the advantages is that paraffin wax is extremely easy to remove from the material, since it disappears completely when boiled in ordinary soapy water. Another advantage is that if you are working with a tjanting you will get very exact, sharp outlines.

The one disadvantage of paraffin wax is that it does not cover large surfaces completely satisfactorily. It should therefore only be used for covering and cracking small surfaces.

The method of procedure is the same as for wax batik (see page 54), apart from the fact that the temperature should be between 120°C and 130°C, and the dye bath should not exceed 30°C. You will therefore have to reckon with a longer dyeing time to achieve the desired strength of colour.

If you are using several dye baths, boil the material for 5 minutes between each bath, adding 1 dessertspoonful of soap flakes per 2 pints (1 litre) of water.

Use boiling water for the first rinse to remove any remains of paraffin wax from the material. After the last dyeing it is advisable to wait about 24 hours before boiling the material.

Paraffin wax is even easier to use on material that has been washed, dried and ironed. It can also be used with printing blocks.

Empty can with wooden clothes pegs. The can is used for melting bits of candle.

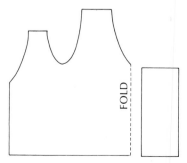

Paper pattern for the bag above.

Appendix

A useful guide for blending dyes

One-bath dye suggestions

Combinations	Resulting colour
1 g violet 1½ g dark pink (peony)	dark purple
1 g cyclamen (reddish violet) 1 g medium brown (coffee)	reddish violet
1½ g dark pink (peony) ½ g cyclamen (reddish violet)	reddish violet
2 g vermilion 2 g dark pink (peony)	dark reddish
2 g dark pink 1 g lemon yellow	strong red
1 g khaki colour 2 g dark pink (peony)	dark ruby red
2 g vermilion 1 g chestnut brown	reddish brown
2 g vermilion 1 g dark orange	reddish yellow
1 g dark orange 1 g chestnut brown	strong orange
1 g cyclamen ¾ g dark orange	sienna
1 g dark orange 2 g medium brown (coffee)	yellowish brown

1½ g lemon yellow 2½ g medium brown (coffee)	olive brown
1 g dark orange 2 g khaki colour	bronze colour
½ g emerald green 2½ g lemon yellow	brilliant green
1 g emerald green 1 g dark pink	grass green
1½ g cornflower blue ½ g dark orange	olive green

1 g = approx $\frac{1}{28}$ oz

Suggestions for two-dye combinations

1 g poppy	first bath
3 g dark pink (peony)	second bath
½ g dark orange	first bath
2 g vermilion and 1 g dark orange	second bath (blended colour)
⅛ g cyclamen (reddish violet) and ⅓ g dark pink (peony)	first bath (blended colour)
½ g vermilion and 1 g dark pink (peony)	second bath (blended colour)
⅙ g cyclamen (reddish violet) and $\frac{1}{16}$ g violet	first bath (blended colour)

½ g cornflower blue and
      cyclamen
      (reddish violet) and
$\frac{1}{16}$ g black
	second bath (blended colour)

¼ g dark orange and ⅛ g emerald green	first bath (blended colour)
1½ g turquoise green and ⅛ g cornflower blue	second bath (blended colour)
½ g turquoise green	first bath
¾ g violet and ⅛ g black	second bath (blended colour)
½ g emerald green and ¼ g medium brown (coffee)	first bath (blended colour)
1 g turquoise green and ¼ g cornflower blue	second bath (blended colour)
½ g dark orange	first bath
1 g dark orange and ¼ g black	second bath (blended colour)
1 g turquoise	first bath
1 g violet and ½ g emerald green	second bath (blended colour)
¼ g turquoise green	first bath
1 g cornflower blue and 1 g khaki colour	second bath (blended colour)
1 g dark orange and ⅛ g black	first bath (blended colour)
1½ g cornflower blue and ½ g dark orange	second bath (blended colour)
½ g vermilion and ¼ g dark orange	first bath (blended colour)
3 g chestnut brown and ¼ g black	second bath (blended colour)
¼ g emerald green	first bath
½ g violet and 1 g cornflower blue	second bath (blended colour)
1 g olive green	first bath
1½ g cornflower blue and ¼ g black	second bath (blended colour)

1 g turquoise green	first bath
1½ g medium brown (coffee)	second bath
½ g cornflower blue	first bath
½ g black	second bath
½ g black (grey)	first bath
3 g black	second bath
½ g cornflower blue	first bath
½ g violet and 1 g cornflower blue	second bath (blended colour)
⅛ g violet and ¼ g cornflower blue	first bath (blended colour)
¾ g cornflower blue and ¾ g cyclamen (reddish violet)	second bath (blended colour)
¼ g cyclamen (reddish violet) and ¼ g medium brown (coffee)	first bath (blended colour)
1 g violet and 1½ g dark pink (peony)	second bath (blended colour)
4 g medium brown (coffee)	first bath
4 g black	second bath

1 g = approx ¹⁄₂₈ oz

Suppliers in Great Britain

Dylon International Ltd.,
139 Sydenham Road,
London S.E.26

Dylon Multipurpose, Dylon Cold, Dylon Liquid dyes and Procion M in small and large quantities. Also chemicals needed for dyeing.

Skilbeck Brothers Ltd.,
Bagnall House,
55-57 Glengall Road,
London S.E.15
(distributors on behalf of ICI)

Supply auxiliary chemicals and the following dyes: Caledon vat dyes (a "Standard Pack" containing twelve 1 oz size bottles is available). Soledon (solubilized vat). Procion "MX" reactive dyes. Solamine Fast. Most of these are supplied in minimum 1 kilo packs and orders will be despatched to all parts of the world.

Dryad Handicraft Ltd.,
Northgates,
Leicester

Arts and Crafts Unlimited,
49 Shelton Street,
London W.C.2

Tjantings, brushes, beeswax etc.

Joshua Hoyle and Sons
(Manchester) Ltd.,
12 Bow Lane,
London E.C.4

Bradley Textiles Ltd.,
15 Stott Street,
Nelson,
Lancashire

Fabrics suitable for batik work.

Emil Adler, 46 Mortimer Street, London W.1	Fabrics suitable for batik work.
Johnsons of Hendon, Radlett Road, Colney Street, St. Albans, Hertfordshire	Indicator papers in boxes of 150.

Suppliers in the USA and Canada

Craftool Dyes for Batik,
Wood-Ridge, New Jersey 07075

Dyes.

Dupont de Nemours Co. Inc.,
50 Page Road,
Clifton, New Jersey

Direct and acid dyes.

Kelco Co.,
75 Terminal Avenue,
Clark, New Jersey

Keltex.

Screen Process Supplies
Manufacturing Co.,
1199 East 12 Street,
Oakland 6, California

Inko vat dyes.

Fezandie and Sperrle Inc.,
103 Lafayette Street,
New York, N.Y. 10013

Allied Chemical Corporation,
National Aniline Division,
40 Rector Street,
New York, N.Y.

Aniline and aljo batik dyes.

ICI Organics Inc.,
55 Canal Street,
Providence,
Rhode Island 02901

Synthrapol SP, Procion M and
Dylon Cold dyes.

Carbic-Hoechst Corporation,
Sheffield Street,
Mountainside, New Jersey

Indigisol and Anthrasol dyes.

Farquahar Fabric Dyes,
Box 1008, Station A,
Toronto 116,
Canada

Reactive dyes: Dylon Cold and
Procion M.

Geigy Chemical Company,
P.O. Box 430,
Yonkers, New York

Tinolite products.

Winsor and Newton Inc.,
555 Winsor Drive,
Secaucus,
New Jersey 07094

Sou-Tex Chemical Co. Inc.,
Mt Holly,
North Carolina 28120

Cassofix FRN-300, fixing agent
for direct and acid dyes.

Most department stores sell the household dyes Rit and Tintex.

Norman Ceramics Co. Inc.,
252 Mamaroneck Avenue,
Mamaroneck, New York

Waxes.

Craftool Dyes for Batik,
Wood-Ridge,
New Jersey 07075

Waxes and tjantings.

Index